RELIGIOUS INTOLERANCE

Jewish Immigrants Come to America
(1881-1914)

Jeremy Thornton

ROSEN CLASSROOM
PRIMARYSOURCE

Rosen Classroom Books & Materials

New York

For my grandfather, Gilbert Thornton

Published in 2004 by The Rosen Publishing Group, Inc.
29 East 21st Street, New York, NY 10010

First Edition

Editor: Rachel O'Connor
Book Design: Emily Muschinske
Layout Design: Mike Donnellan

Photo Credits: Cover and title page, pp. 4 (bottom), 7 (right), 12, 15 (bottom), 16, 19, 20 (top) Culver Pictures; p. 4 (top) © Bettmann/Corbis; pp. 7 (top), 15 (top) from the Archives of the YIVO Institute for Jewish Research; p. 7 (left) map by Eric DePalo; p. 8 (top) © Hulton-Deutsch Collection/Corbis; p. 8 (bottom) © Corbis; p. 11 (top) Library of Congress Geography and Map Division; p. 11 (bottom) © Hulton/Archive/Getty Images; p. 20 (left and right) Ira M. Beck Memorial Archives, Penrose Library, University of Denver.

Thornton, Jeremy.
Religious intolerance : Jewish immigrants come to America (1881–1914) / Jeremy Thornton.— 1st ed.
    v. cm. — (Primary sources of immigration and migration in America)
Includes bibliographical references and index.
Contents: Choosing America — The Jews in Russia — Turn for the worse — The Jews immigrate — Difficult passage — Voyage and arrival — Immigrant aid societies — Peddling and garment work — Life in the cities — Success and choice in America.
"Includes bibliographical references and index."
ISBN 0-8239-6834-0 (library binding) — ISBN 0-8239-8960-7 (pbk.)
1. Jews—Persecutions—Russia—Juvenile literature. 2. Russia—Ethnic relations—Juvenile literature. 3. Jews—United States—History—20th century—Juvenile literature. 4. Jews, Russian—United States—History—Juvenile literature. 5. Immigrants—United States—History—20th century—Juvenile literature. 6. United States—Ethnic relations—Juvenile literature. [1. Jews—Persecutions—Russia. 2. Russia—Ethnic relations. 3. Jews—United States—History—20th century. 4. Immigrants—United States—History—20th century. 5. United States—Emigration and immigration—History. 6. Russia—Emigration and immigration—History. 7. United States—Ethnic relations.] I. Title. II. Series.
DS135.R7 T48 2004
973'.04924047—dc21

2003004578

Manufactured in the United States of America

Contents

Left: *In this print, Jewish refugees are on a boat bound for New York.*

Below: *Ellis Island opened in 1892 as America's new immigration center. Castle Garden, the first center, could not handle the growing numbers of immigrants.*

Choosing America

Throughout its history, America has been known as a symbol of choice and freedom. Since the late 1700s, many American citizens have been free to follow their religious and political beliefs. They have been free to move from place to place and to settle and work where they please. People in countries all over the world heard of this freedom and were drawn to America. Some immigrants came from places where they had no say in how their government ran their country. Others came from places where they were persecuted for their religious beliefs. From 1881 to 1914, about two million Jews came to America from Russia. They came in search of political and religious freedom.

The Jews in Russia

Jewish settlements have existed all over the world, including in parts of Asia, Africa, and Europe, for thousands of years. During the 1700s, there were large Jewish communities in Russia. This was a time when Russia was becoming a powerful empire by conquering neighboring lands. It was also a time when anti-Semitism in Russia was widespread. By the early 1800s, the Russian government had created laws that limited the Jewish people's rights. For example, Jews were only allowed to live in a certain area, known as the Pale of Settlement. Fueled by the anti-Semitism that existed, Russians sometimes attacked Jews. These attacks were known as pogroms.

This map shows what the Pale of Settlement looked like from 1835 to 1917. By 1885, there were more than four million Jews living in the Pale.

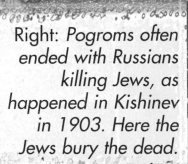

Right: *Pogroms often ended with Russians killing Jews, as happened in Kishinev in 1903. Here the Jews bury the dead.*

BALTIC SEA

KOVNO

VITEBSK

● Moscow

GERMANY

SUVALKI

VILNA

PLOZK

LOMZHA

MOGILEV

KALISZ

WARSAW

HRODNA

MINSK

RUSSIA

SYEDLETS

PIOTRKÓW

RADOM

LUBLIN

CHERNIGOV

KIELCE

VOLHYNIA

AUSTRIA-HUNGARY

PODOLIA

KIEV

POLTAVA

BESSARABIA

EKATERINOSLAV

KHERSON

ROMANIA

TAURIDA

BLACK SEA

Above: *Here Russians attack a Jewish house in Konnovino in 1884, showing the anti-Semitism that existed.*

7

Left: *Pictured is Alexander II, who was czar of Russia from 1855 until 1881. Following his death, he was succeeded by his second son, Alexander III.*

Below: *The terrorists who murdered Alexander II were hanged in St. Petersburg, Russia, for their crime.*

Things Get Worse in Russia

On March 13, 1881, terrorists killed Russian czar Alexander II. After his death, anti-Semitism became even more widespread. Many Russians blamed the Jews for his death because one of the terrorists was a Jew. In the unrest that followed the czar's death, pogroms became more common. Hundreds of Jews were killed during this time. In May 1882, the Russian government used the violence and unrest as an excuse to pass a series of laws. These laws further discriminated against the Jews. These so-called Temporary Laws included reducing the area of the Pale of Settlement by 10 percent. Jews were still forbidden from living outside this area. Also, Jews were not allowed to work as lawyers or in government.

Getting Out of Russia

As life became more unpleasant for the Russian Jews, many of them decided they could no longer live in Russia. They began to hear stories about the opportunities that existed in America. However, leaving Russia was not easy in the late 1800s. The Russian government made it hard for people to get passports to leave the country. It was even harder for the Jews, whose movement the government especially tried to restrict. Officially, Jews were restricted from travel. Unofficially, government officials would help Jews get passports for a certain amount of money, known as a bribe. Many Jews were poor and had to leave Russia illegally, sneaking across the Russian border.

Once out of Russia the immigrants had to cross Europe, usually through Germany. From Europe they sailed across the Atlantic Ocean to America.

Below: *Here a group of Russian and Polish immigrants are on a ship heading to America from Europe. This picture is from the early 1900s.*

Arrival in America

   In the late 1800s, it took immigrants between two and three weeks to cross the Atlantic in steamships. Western Europeans traveled in cabins because they usually had more money. Jewish immigrants had to travel below deck because they could not afford the more expensive tickets. They slept on iron bunk beds padded with straw. Most of them were too seasick to eat, and there was not a lot of drinking water. When the ships arrived in America, the immigrants were taken to Castle Garden, or to Ellis Island after 1891. Those two islands were used by the U.S. government as centers to receive immigrants.

Pictured here at Ellis Island are officials giving immigrants a medical exam, looking for signs of disease. Those who were found to be suffering from diseases were sent back to Europe.

Immigrant Aid Societies

The Jews in western European countries, such as Germany, France, and England, and in America wanted to help their fellow Jews escape Russia. They created societies in Europe and in America, such as the Hebrew Immigrant Aid Society and the Jewish Colonization Society. These societies collected money from Jews all over the world to help the Russian immigrants pay for their journey to America. They arranged for Jews in various European cities to bring the Russian Jews from the train stations to the ships heading for America. In America, the societies helped the immigrants by operating kitchens to feed the new arrivals.

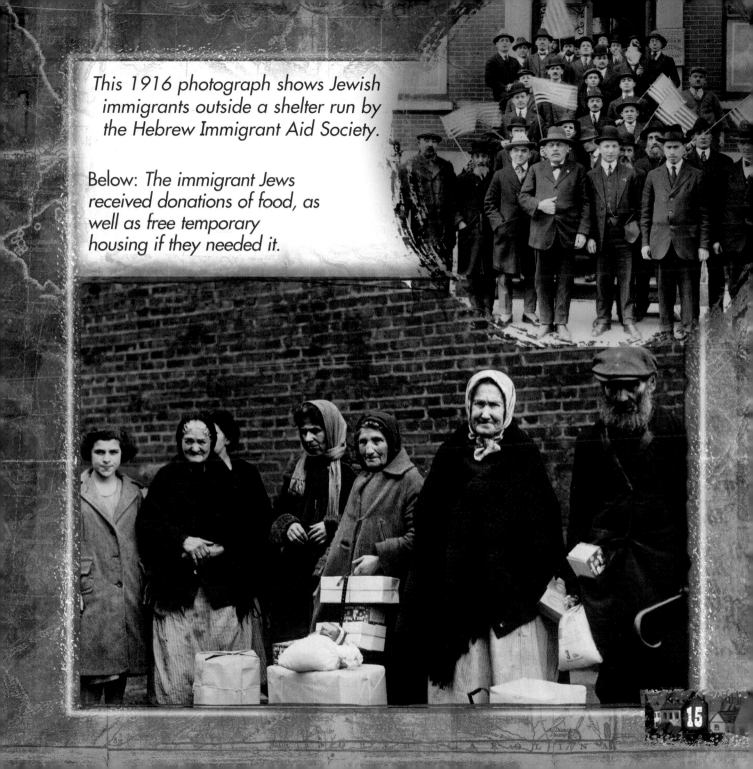

This 1916 photograph shows Jewish immigrants outside a shelter run by the Hebrew Immigrant Aid Society.

Below: *The immigrant Jews received donations of food, as well as free temporary housing if they needed it.*

Left: Many Russian Jews found work in the sweatshops of lower Manhattan. They learned how to sew, cut, and press clothing, for little pay.

Below: Shown is a Jewish peddler in New York City around 1915. Some peddlers did well, but most peddled only until they found a better job.

Jobs in America

Many Jews from Russia found work as peddlers. Immigrant aid societies or other friendly Jews in America sometimes gave the newly arrived immigrants some money to buy goods to sell. The peddler would then walk around carrying his goods or pushing them on a cart. Other Jewish immigrants found work making clothes, which was easy to learn. The garments were made in sweatshops, which were small, crowded, dirty rooms. The sweatshops were often located in the tenements where Russian Jews lived. Jews usually worked long hours to make a living, often 12 to 15 hours per day. The rooms were hot in the summer and cold in the winter. Other Russian Jews found work in factories, on an assembly line.

Life in the Cities

Most of the Jews who came to America from Russia in the late 1800s settled in such port cities as New York, Boston, and Philadelphia, where the steamships landed. By the time the Russian Jews arrived in the 1880s, there were already about 250,000 Jews from other parts of the world living in America. Most were settled in New York City. The Russian Jews found jobs and Jewish communities in New York and in other cities. However, even though they found jobs and a sense of community, there was a period of adjustment for many of the Russian Jews. They worked hard to exist, often living in crowded, rundown, and dirty housing.

In the early 1900s, the Lower East Side of Manhattan had a large Jewish community. Rows of tenement buildings lined the streets in this poor area.

Left: *This document, from the Torah, is called the Pentateuch, and is used for worship in the synagogues.*

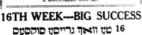

PALM THEATRE
3116 WEST COLFAX AVENUE
L. JOSEPHSON, Mgr.   N. WEINSTEIN, Stage Mgr.
H. HOFFENBERG, Artist Mgr.

16TH WEEK---BIG SUCCESS

MME. GERBER   H. HOFFENBERG   N. WEINSTEIN   A. FELDSTEIN   MADAME M. COOPER

Tuesday Night, December 25th
Xmas night
Shown the first time in Denver. A most wonderful melodram.

"The Second Wife"

in 4 acts with songs and dances

Wednesday Night, December 26th Ladies Free ## "THE BLIND LOVE" in four acts with songs and dances	**Friday Night, December 28th** Delightful Jewish Vaudeville, Including New Songs—Sketches and A Feature Movie

Ladies Free   **Saturday Night, December 29 h**

"A Sister's Sacrifice"
In four acts with songs and dances

Sunday Night, December 30th
The first appearance in Denver of the well known Jewish actor who is recognized as one of the best actors on the Jewish Stage.

SAMUEL MORRIS
WATCH OUR ANNOUNCEMENT!

ATTENTION PLEASE!
A testimonial performance will be given Sunday evening, Jan. 13th in honor of our leading man and character performer, Mr. Nathan Weinstein.
Shylock or the Merchant of Venice is the play that Mr. Weinstein has selected for this evening.

Reserve Your Seats by Phone - - - - - - - Champa 1943-R
Admission 50c and 85c, including War Tax.

Above: *This advertisement for a Jewish Theater is written partly in Yiddish, a language spoken by Jews from eastern Europe.*

20

Children and Community

The Russian Jews saw education as a way to escape the hard conditions. Parents worked long hours and saved money so that their children could go to school instead of having to work like other children at the time. The Russian Jews placed a lot of faith in their children. They did everything they could to make sure their children's lives would one day be easier than their own lives were.

Jews worshiped together in synagogues. They also watched Yiddish theater together to provide relief from their hard living conditions. Yiddish theater, which was a very popular type of drama performed in the Yiddish language, strengthened the Jewish sense of community.

This class picture was taken on the steps of the Yeshivas Etz Chaim School in Denver, Colorado, where some of the Jewish immigrants settled.

Success and Choice in America

Although life for the new immigrants was hard in America, it was still better than life in Russia. They joined the Jewish communities that already existed, making them stronger. The Jews in America worked hard to make a better life for themselves and their children, and it paid off. Many became successful in their new homes. Famous descendants of Russian Jews include songwriter Cole Porter and writer Saul Bellow. Other descendants became great actors, such as Dustin Hoffman, or sportsmen, such as Hank Greenberg. Some, such as Emma Goldman, were political activists. Jews were free to choose how to live, to worship, and to work. They proved that America was indeed a land of freedom and choice.

Glossary

activists (AK-tih-vists) People who take action for their beliefs.

adjustment (uh-JUST-ment) Changing to fit new conditions.

anti-Semitism (an-tee-SEH-mih-tih-zum) Meanness toward Jews.

czar (ZAR) A Russian king.

descendants (dih-SEN-dents) People who are born of a certain family or group.

discriminated (dis-KRIH-mih-nayt-id) To have treated a person unfairly just because he or she is different.

disease (duh-ZEEZ) Illness or sickness.

donations (doh-NAY-shunz) Gifts of money, food, or help.

immigrants (IH-muh-grints) People who move to a new country from another country.

passports (PAS-ports) Official papers needed to leave and to enter a country other than your own.

peddler (PED-lur) A person who travels around and sells things.

persecuted (PER-sih-kyoot-ed) Attacked for one's race or beliefs.

refugees (reh-fyoo-JEEZ) People who leave their country to find safety.

restrict (rih-STRIKT) To keep within limits.

symbol (SIM-bul) An object or a picture that stands for something else.

synagogues (SIH-nih-gogz) Jewish places of worship.

temporary (TEM-puh-rer-ee) Lasting for a short amount of time.

tenements (TEN-uh-ments) Buildings with many floors and with many families living on each level.

violence (VY-lens) Strong force used to cause harm.

Index

Primary Sources

Page 4. Top. Jewish refugees from Russia passing the Statue of Liberty. 1892. **Page 7. Top.** After the pogrom in Kishinev in 1903, men stand behind the dead on stretchers, covered with desecrated Torah scrolls. **Right.** Attack by the populace on a Jewish house at Konnovino. 1884. **Page 8. Bottom.** Five of the six conspirators, found guilty of planning the assassination of the emperor Alexander II, which took place on March 16, 1881, stand on the scaffold in St. Petersburg waiting to be hanged. The execution of the sixth conspirator was delayed due to her pregnancy. **Page 11. Top.** Map of Europe. 1898. **Bottom.** Polish and Russian immigrants ride in the steerage of a ship heading to America from Europe. Circa 1905. **Page 15. Top.** Jewish immigrants outside a shelter run by the Hebrew Immigrant Aid Society (HIAS) in New York City. 1916. **Page 16. Top.** A Jewish man works at a sewing machine in the sweatshops on New York City. 1898. In places such as these, the Jews learned the basics of the garment industry: sewing and basting, cutting and pressing. **Bottom.** Jewish peddler on Manhattan's Lower East Side. Circa 1915. **Page 19.** Tenement buildings and an outdoor market on Rivington Street, New York City. 1905. **Page 20. Left.** Advertisement for the Jewish theater at the Palm Theater, Denver, Colorado. It appeared in the *Denver Jewish News* in 1923. The theater was established by the Jewish Theatrical Company, organized by the Josephon family.

Web Sites

Due to the changing nature of Internet links, PowerKids Press has developed an online list of Web sites related to the subject of this book. This site is updated regularly. Please use this link to access the list:

      www.powerkidslinks.com/psima/relint/